REVITALIZE YOUR COMPANY WITH
INTERNAL CONSULTING EXPERTISE

ANTHONY GUIDO | KIRK ATKINSON | MIKE LARKIN

Published in 1999 by Stoddart Publishing Co. Limited
34 Lesmill Road, Toronto, Canada M3B 2T6

Distributed in Canada by General Distribution Services Limited
325 Humber College Blvd., Toronto, Ontario M9W 7C3
Tel. (416) 213-1919   Fax (416) 213-1917
Email Customer.Service@ccmailgw.genpub.com

Distributed in the U.S. by General Distribution Services Inc.
85 River Rock Drive, Suite 202, Buffalo, New York 14207
Toll-free tel. 1-800-805-1083 Toll-free fax 1-800-481-6207
Email gdsinc@genpub.com

03 02 01 00 99 1 2 3 4 5

Cataloguing in Publication Data

Guido, Anthony, 1964–
ICE : revitalize your company with Internal Consulting Expertise

ISBN 0-7737-6026-1

1. Business consultants.   I. Atkinson, Kirk, 1958–   .
II. Larkin, Mike, 1950–   .   III. Title.

HD69.C6G84 1999   658.4'6
C98-932659-X

Cover design: Bill Douglas @ The Bang
Design and typesetting: Kinetics Design & Illustration

Printed and bound in Canada

To our wives and children
for their love and support

Contents

The ICE Man

*J*oe looked at the financial reports that moments ago had been handed to him by Kent Waters, his chief financial officer. His company's situation was worsening despite Joe's and his management team's best efforts to turn around what was clearly now a rapidly sinking ship. He keyed the intercom and waited for the familiar tone. "Rachel, would you please call an emergency meeting of our executive team? I want them gathered in the boardroom at 5 today."

"Shall I say what it's about, Joe?"

He sighed before replying. "If they're as smart as I think they are, they already know."

At precisely 5 P.M. Joe Tanner, the president and principal shareholder of Tanner Enterprises, entered the beautifully adorned boardroom joining his office. His entire senior management team was in the room already and had seated themselves around the impressive oak table. A couple of them acknowledged Joe with a quiet greeting, but the rest of the team sat silently as he took his customary place at the head of the table. He cleared his throat.

"By now, I believe each of you has received our third-quarter results." Kent Waters nodded. "We're in trouble, gang," Joe continued, "and I think we've run out of options. Unless someone has a few brilliant ideas I think we're looking at massive layoffs and maybe even the end of Tanner Enterprises." In the history of his company there had been layoffs, but Joe had never talked about insolvency. His message was very clear. The company was in dire financial straits.

Bill Conrad, Tanner's vice-president of marketing, broke the silence. "Joe, I really think things are going to turn around once we launch our new Platinum software. My marketing consultant is projecting a three-point gain in share within a year."

"Bill, if we don't do something now, we'll never launch the Platinum line. Our cash flow is so bad that we're in danger of missing our next payroll."

Kent agreed. "Joe's right. We're overextended at every financial institution we're dealing with and, quite frankly, none of them are prepared to extend us more credit. Joe and I are meeting with our financiers three days from now. Unless we have a new story to tell them, I'm afraid they may opt to close us down."

Dyson Lane, Tanner's vice-president of human resources, shook her head in disgust. "I don't understand how this can be happening."

"It's not like we didn't see it coming, Dyson," said

Joe. "We've known about our problems for quite some time now."

"And it isn't that we haven't tried to address them," added Chelsea Bain, Tanner's vice-president of strategic planning.

"That's what I don't understand," said Jay Cameron, Tanner's vice-president of information technology. "We turned the company on its ear during the last year in order to solve our problems and things are worse now than when we started."

"We only did what our strategic planning consultants advised us to do," offered Chelsea.

"Exactly. And the year before that," Jay continued, "we reorganized completely in anticipation of the industry changes we knew were coming."

"Our industry advisers said we had to reorganize or we wouldn't survive," said Ben Riley, Tanner's vice-president of sales.

Kent chimed in, "They were only half right. We aren't going to survive at the rate we're going. My financial consultant is convinced there's no other way to get out of this."

Joe looked directly at his CFO. "I'm afraid Kent is right. We have to cut every department in half and we have to do it now. You each have forty-eight hours to decide which employees you want to release. I'll also need a detailed summary of the implications of these cuts on your respective departments. We'll reconvene here in the boardroom two days from now at 5 P.M.

The executive team filed out of the boardroom quietly. Joe watched them go, then retreated to his office. He couldn't remember a worse day in his business life. He took a deep breath and let it out slowly. He needed a workout. It would help him think clearly.

Joe was twenty minutes into his StairMaster workout when his thoughts were interrupted by a familiar voice. "So, what gives, Tanner? I've been climbing away beside you for almost ten minutes and you haven't even acknowledged my presence. And besides, why aren't you on the squash courts where you belong?"

Joe turned to his right and saw the smiling face of his good friend and frequent squash partner, Wally. "Oh, hi, Wally. Sorry, I didn't notice you."

"You look like you're off in never-never land. Is everything okay?"

Joe tried to smile but couldn't quite pull it off. "Yeah, I mean . . . just some work-related stuff, Wally. The kind of stuff you and I agreed never to talk about, remember?"

"I remember." Wally and Joe had made a pact years before to avoid talking about work issues at the gym when they met for their regular squash game. Their friendship did not extend outside the boundaries of the club, so they had, in fact, never talked about work.

"So . . ." Joe shrugged.

Wally did not reply. After a minute or so, he said,

"Joe, I've known you for a long time and even though our friendship has been based on our mutual love of squash, I've shared enough beers with you in the lounge to know that things are not good for you right now."

"They've been better," Joe agreed reluctantly.

"Then it's time to break our rule. Tell me what's going on and maybe I can help."

"Wally, I think I'm beyond help."

"Then it can't hurt to let me try, right?"

Joe managed a thin smile. "Okay. Meet me in the lounge in about forty minutes and I'll tell you my tale of woe."

"I'll be there," said Wally as he climbed down from the StairMaster. "I'm on the court with Nelson in about five minutes and it never takes me more than thirty to whip his butt."

"*You* beat Nelson?"

"Not yet, but it makes for a good story."

The two friends laughed, then Joe watched Wally walk off in the direction of the squash courts. Joe doubted Wally could help him. Joe didn't even know what Wally did for a living. Still, it wouldn't hurt to share his problems with his old squash buddy. If nothing else, talking about the state of Tanner Enterprises would allow him to vent some of his frustration.

"So, did you win?"

Wally chuckled. "Are you kidding? He killed me. He

always does, but I love playing against him. He keeps me sharp enough to consistently beat guys like you."

"In your dreams," Joe laughed.

Wally sat across from his friend. "So, spill your guts."

Joe ran a hand through his thick, gray hair, then took a deep breath and let it out slowly. "Where to begin?"

Joe talked for nearly an hour and Wally listened attentively, occasionally scribbling in a little notebook he had taken out of his gym bag. Finally, Joe had told all. Now, it was Wally's turn to speak.

"Joe, how often have you been injured while playing squash?"

Joe looked puzzled. "Every once in a while, but I don't see what —"

"And how do you treat an injury?"

"Well, I usually put ice on it."

"Right. And that's exactly what you need to do to Tanner Enterprises. You should ICE all those problems your firm has."

Joe looked at his friend and shook his head. "Wally, maybe this was a mistake. This is not help —"

Again Wally interrupted. "Joe, do you know what I do for a living?"

"No, I don't."

"I'm the founder and principal shareholder of Walden Chase Incorporated."

Joe was dumbfounded. "*You're Walden Chase*?"

Walden Chase was the founder of an extremely successful multinational company. The reclusive man was considered one of the foremost business geniuses of his time. The small, thin, bespectacled man seated in front of Joe looked nothing like the Walden Chase who occasionally appeared in the nation's business magazines. Walden Chase smiled. "I'm 'Wally' to my friends."

"I had no idea."

"And neither does anybody else at this club. So let's keep it that way, okay?"

"Sure."

"Now, as for Tanner Enterprises, as I said before, you need to ICE your problems, Joe. It's the only way for you to save your sinking ship."

"Wally, this doesn't make sense to me."

"I don't expect it to now, but it will. Tomorrow morning I want you to fire every single consultant you have working for Tanner and when that's done come to my office. I'll expect you there by nine."

"Fire our consultants? Wally, we have some of the best minds in the country working on our behalf. I don't know if it makes sense to just fire them."

"Joe, listen to me. I'm one of the richest men in the world. I started my first business when I was twelve, and I had amassed a small fortune by the time I was twenty-four. In fact, at that time Walden Chase was about the size that Tanner Enterprises is today. And you know what? I almost lost the whole company, everything I had worked so hard to build, by doing the same things you are probably doing today. What saved me was ICE.

It can save you, too, Joe, if you let it. But first you have to trust me. I want you to fire your consultants and be at my office by nine tomorrow morning. Can you do that, Joe?"

Joe sighed. He thought the idea was bizarre but he reluctantly agreed. "Consider it done, Wally."

"Great." Wally stood and reached across the table to shake his friend's hand. "You've just taken the first step toward saving Tanner Enterprises. I'll see you tomorrow."

2

Understanding ICE

*F*irst, thanks to each of you for adjusting your schedules to join this early morning conference call. I know you are working feverishly to prepare for tomorrow afternoon's meeting." Joe waited for a response from his executive team, but was met with silence. He was already beginning to regret his decision. He took a deep breath and continued.

"I've made a decision and I wanted to tell all of you about it directly, so I arranged for this call. Um . . . I want . . . I've decided to fire all of the firm's consultants and I'd like you to act on my decision today."

"You can't be serious, Joe!" protested Bill Conrad. "My god, I've got a whole team of consultants developing strategy for the Platinum product launch. I can't just turf these guys."

"You're going to have to trust me on this one, Bill. Please, just do what I'm asking you to."

"Joe, it's Chelsea. I really don't understand what's going on here. Firing our consultants at a time like this seems, well . . . risky. Is there something else happening that we should know about?"

"There is, Chelsea, but I can't really explain it in detail right now. I've received some advice from a well-respected member of the business community and —"

Bill interrupted, obviously frustrated. "*Advice*, Joe? Gee, from a consultant? Is *he* getting fired, too?"

Joe was a patient, caring leader but he had his limits. Still, he kept his composure, and answered as calmly as he could. "Bill, I know your comments are based on genuine concern for this company. I appreciate it. However, this is not a subject I'm prepared to debate. I'm directing you and everybody else on this call to fire every consultant we have on the payroll, and to do it today."

Bill apologized, and the call went quiet. Joe had made his point. The consultants would certainly be fired, for reasons nobody, including Joe, understood.

Later, as he wheeled into the parking lot of Walden Chase, Joe said aloud, "This ICE thing had better be good."

❖

The first thing Joe noticed when he arrived at Walden Chase's reception area was laughter. It was a sound he hadn't heard at the offices of Tanner Enterprises for quite a while, and he realized how much he had missed it. He approached the receptionist, who had stopped her kibitzing with some nearby co-workers to greet him.

"Mr. Tanner, welcome to Walden Chase. My name's Adrienne, and it's a pleasure to meet you."

Joe shook her hand. This was certainly the warmest greeting he had ever received by a receptionist in all his years in business. It made him feel really good. "Nice to meet you, Adrienne. How did you know who I am?"

She grinned. "Look behind you."

Joe turned to see a large multimedia bulletin board inset on the wall above the front doors. His picture was among the images of three other people, each of whom had appointments at 9 A.M. An on-screen banner above each digital photo read, "Welcome to Walden Chase. Enjoy your day!" Joe looked back at Adrienne. "How —"

"As soon as Wally registered your appointment on our local area network, I checked out your Internet site and found your photo. Wally's notes indicated your appointment wasn't a confidential one, so I scanned your photo and displayed it."

"I'm impressed."

"Well, my job is to receive our guests, right? I can't receive you very well if I don't know anything about you, can I?"

Joe agreed. "I guess not. It's really quite a good idea."

"Thanks. It's an ICE original."

"ICE? Really?"

"ICE," replied Adrienne. "It's changed our company."

Now Joe was really intrigued. The *receptionist* knew about ICE? And she attributed the innovative reception area to it? "Is Mr. Chase ready to see me?"

"Of course. We keep every appointment, internal or external, on time. Promptness is a way of life at Walden Chase."

"Let me guess. ICE?"

"ICE," she smiled. "You're a quick study."

"I hope so, Adrienne."

"Come with me. Wally's waiting for you."

As they left the reception area, Adrienne yelled, "Tag!" As she did so, a nearby employee jumped up from her desk and hurried toward the reception area, giving Adrienne a high-five as she passed her. Adrienne looked back at Joe. "We never leave our reception area unstaffed, even for a minute."

"So you just yell tag?"

"That's right. It's my way of letting people know I need to be relieved from a customer-facing duty for a few minutes. Customer activity always takes priority. It's a Walden Chase rule."

"ICE?"

"ICE."

Joe followed Adrienne through a maze of workstations until they arrived at a centrally located meeting area. Wally was sitting in a comfortable easy chair in the center of the room. The chair was one of many, creating a relaxed, large family room effect. Wally looked up as they approached.

"Joe, welcome." He rose from his seat to greet his guest.

"Thanks. It's nice to be here. And Adrienne ensured I was given a warm welcome."

Wally smiled at his receptionist. "Thanks, Adrienne. I'm not surprised, Joe. She's an outstanding individual. We're proud to have her on the team." Adrienne thanked Wally for the compliment and returned to her workstation.

"Adrienne was telling me how ICE helped her in her job as your receptionist."

"ICE has helped all of us."

"So, what is ICE? I'm dying to know."

"Patience, my friend. You'll know soon enough, but first I have to get a better understanding of the problems facing Tanner Enterprises."

"Okay. I gave you an overview yesterday at the club. I think I hit all the high points. What else do you need to know?"

"Quite a bit. The information you gave me yesterday was excellent, but more than anything it prompted some questions." Wally waved a paper in his right hand. It was clear to Joe that Wally had prepared for his visit.

"Ask away."

"Did you fire your consultants?"

"First thing this morning. Despite the protests of my management team."

"They were upset?"

"Every one of them."

"And why do you think your executive team was upset?"

Joe thought for a moment. "They rely on the consultants to help them do their jobs."

"To help them make decisions?"

"Exactly."

"Or to make decisions for them?"

The implication of Wally's question was clear. Were Tanner's consultants actually making decisions for his people, or were they merely guiding them in their decision making? "I guess they do a little of both," answered Joe.

"Can you think of an example of when a consultant made a decision on behalf of Tanner Enterprises?"

"Well, several come to mind. I guess the most important one had to do with a restructuring we completed last year. One of our business units was a little bit out of control. It was causing some internal grief, so a guy I use quite a bit conducted a business unit review for me and he recommended —"

Wally interrupted. "He *decided*."

Joe laughed. "Okay, he *decided* to disband the business unit and overlay its activities on the rest of the company, which is organized along functional lines of responsibility."

"So you acted on the consultant's decision. Did the internal conflict that this unit was creating disappear with the restructuring?"

"There was a lot of bitterness from the members of the renegade business unit at first, but eventually it died down. And the internal conflict went away."

"So the consultant made a good decision?"

"I think so."

"How did the market respond?"

"The internal restructuring was conducted independent of the market. Our goal was to hide it from our customers."

Wally smiled. "Let me get at this another way. What kind of growth was the renegade unit achieving before it was broken up?

"Double-digit."

"What was its share?"

"Thirty percent. Number one in the market."

"What about today?"

"Well, the growth has tailed off a bit. Quite a bit, actually. And, well, our share has slipped to just over twenty-five percent."

"Do you still think the consultant's decision was invisible to the market?"

He had never discussed it with anybody, but in his heart Joe knew that the breakup of the business unit had been a mistake. It had led to the loss of a number of good employees, and, while the internal conflict had disappeared, Tanner Enterprises had lost its momentum in a vibrant emerging market. "We did solve some in-house problems, but the decision to break up the unit was likely the wrong one."

"Joe, I'm not trying to make you feel bad here. Breaking up the renegade unit may very well have been the right decision. While you lost some share and your growth rate diminished, you did solve some internal conflict issues, which can be crippling to a company. My point is that the wrong people made the decision. In matters like this, you need to tap into the minds of the right people in order to increase your chances of making the best decision."

"Okay," said Joe, exasperated. "But who are the *right* people?"

"That's what you're here to discover, Joe. It's the secret to ICE. But before I tell you what ICE is and how it works, I need to know the answer to my other questions." Wally again waved the sheet of paper he held in his right hand. "Will you indulge me?"

"I'm in your capable hands."

"Great." Wally looked at the paper. "Tell me this: What are the three values in your life to which you most subscribe? Also, try and express them in a statement or a phrase if you can."

"Okay. First, I try to maintain a balanced lifestyle. I also do everything in moderation. And live and interact with others in a way that makes them feel better for having been with me."

"What kind of feelings do these values generate in others?"

"Well, I hope they make people want to be with me. Maybe care for me and, in the case of my family and close friends, even love me."

"Good. Now, what are the values to which Tanner Enterprises subscribes?"

Joe looked puzzled. "I'm not sure I understand."

"Companies have values, the same way people do, Joe. Too often, however, companies don't live up to the values they subscribe to because they don't know what those values are. This results in a tremendous imbalance that sees companies behaving in ways inconsistent with their values. When that happens, companies fail."

"That makes a lot of sense. You think we're not operating according to our values."

"I can guarantee it. And when you're not operating according to your values, your Value/Feeling equation is totally out of synch."

"Value/Feeling?"

"Value/Feeling is the foundation of ICE. Once you understand the Value/Feeling dimension and how to apply it to your business, your problems will quickly disappear."

"Really?"

"Really. One last question, Joe. What is the biggest challenge facing Tanner Enterprises today?"

Joe's sky-blue eyes twinkled mischievously. "Do I have to stop at one?"

"Glad to see you haven't lost your sense of humor."

"It's what keeps me going." Joe paused before continuing. "Okay. Our biggest challenge. Let's see . . . how about achieving sustained revenue growth. It seems we have a good year, then a bad year. We can't maintain any kind of momentum in the marketplace, which constantly creates pressure on the business."

"In what way?"

"Well, we always plan for growth and when it doesn't occur, it creates a whole series of problems."

"Such as?"

"Inconsistent cash flow and lack of a stable work-force. When we don't achieve our growth targets, our cash flow suffers and we end up cutting staff to make ends meet. When we cut people, the remaining employees become understandably nervous and, invariably, we end up with a number of resignations as people move to companies they perceive to be more stable. Sometimes they even get jobs at our competitors. That's kind of where we're at right now. Only this time, the problem is even bigger."

"You're being forced to cut resources in order to survive, but that very action limits your ability to grow and recover."

"You've got it."

"How is this affecting your position in the market?" asked Wally.

"It's certainly hurting our image. I know for a fact that it's not as strong as it was in the late 1980s."

"I remember. You were once looked upon as one of the top organizations in the country."

"Yeah, in the glory days."

"What changed?"

"For some reason we lost our ability to be innovative. Also, the incredible pace of *technological change* hurts us so badly, both from an internal systems perspective and in the marketplace."

"Do you face new, more sophisticated competitors?" asked Wally.

"Definitely, and from nontraditional sources. Given the increased and more sophisticated competition we're facing, I guess it's no wonder that we've had difficulty sustaining revenue growth."

"Joe, you can solve all these problems stemming from your inability to sustain revenue growth by applying ICE. Your circumstances are very similar to Walden Chase's before we embraced ICE."

"In what way?"

"We didn't really understand our values and certainly didn't understand our Value/Feeling equation."

"And ICE helped you do that?"

"Absolutely. In fact, why don't we walk you through Walden Chase's situation as a means of illustrating how ICE helped us understand our Value/Feeling equation. Would that be helpful?"

Joe laughed. "What would be most helpful is if you'd tell me what ICE *is!*"

"Come on. Let's take a walk. I want you to meet our vice-president of strategic planning, Sara Daly. Her experience will illustrate how ICE helped Walden Chase understand our values and our Values/Feelings. And on the way, I'll explain what ICE is. I promise."

3

ICE and Your
Value/Feeling Equation

*A*s the men made their way toward the front of the building, Joe heard Adrienne yell "Tag!" As she moved away from her workstation, Wally was the co-worker nearest to her. He gave her a high-five, then settled into the reception area.

"I see that nobody is too big to be behind the front desk at Walden Chase."

"Hey, even if I thought that, do you think I'd have the nerve to tell Adrienne?" Joe laughed, and Wally continued.

"*One team* is one of our guiding values, Joe. It means that every employee chips in to help out when a co-worker needs assistance." Wally glanced at his watch. "I think Adrienne's probably taking a break, so she'll likely be ten minutes or so. Pull up a chair."

Joe seated himself behind the reception desk and beside his friend. He looked at Wally expectantly. "Well?"

"Okay. ICE is an acronym. You probably guessed that. It stands for Internal Consulting Expertise, and it represents a tried-and-true system of solving a company's problems by tapping into the expertise and intelligence in every company. That expertise is the lifeblood knowledge of any company. Unfortunately, most companies don't exploit that resource, most often because they don't know how. Applying ICE solves that dilemma."

"This seems too simple."

"It is and it isn't. The system is simple to apply. Acquiring the discipline to apply it is not. It means embracing a mindset that suggests companies can heal themselves from within."

"Which explains your request that I fire our consultants."

"Exactly. Now, don't misunderstand me. I think consultants can bring value to the business world. In fact, I still use them on occasion. I don't, however, subscribe to the belief that consultants should be hired to try and fix a company's problems. That's the time when most companies hire them and, invariably, what happens is that the consultants generate a whole lot of work by a whole lot of people, and not a whole lot happens. And the very people who should be engaged in fixing the company defer to the consultants."

"We abdicate responsibility." Joe said.

"That's right. And if things don't work out, well, *the consultants messed up*."

"And another consultant is brought in."

Wally chuckled. "I can see you've been there."

The phone rang. Wally answered it, then expertly

directed the call. This gave Joe a moment to think, and he quickly concluded that Wally was right. Tanner Enterprises had not tapped into the expertise within the company. The executive team had assumed all of the responsibility for solving Tanner's problems and, in many instances, had abdicated responsibility by virtue of retaining consultants to solve the company's problems. Maybe ICE was worth a shot.

"Wally, when and where did you learn about ICE?"

"I first learned about ICE from a friend of my father's who mentored me through the early days of Walden Chase."

"Is he still a mentor to you?"

"Unfortunately, he died several years ago. He was a really interesting man who had run a number of successful businesses in his day, mostly in Europe. He had learned about ICE from his father who had developed the system and had used it in the family business for years with great results. In his latter years he spent most of his time mentoring people like me. I guess he didn't want ICE to die when he did."

"And does ICE always work?"

"It's worked for my company and, according to my mentor, ICE has worked in every situation where it was applied with discipline."

Joe was now convinced.

Walden Chase and other companies had proved ICE could work. There was no reason that it couldn't work for Tanner Enterprises.

Adrienne returned to the reception desk. She thanked Wally and the two men continued on to Sara Daly's office.

"I like what I'm hearing, Wally."

"You'll like it even more when Sara walks you through a real situation."

"Understanding our Value/Feeling equation?"

"Right."

Sara Daly's office was as comfortable as the best of family rooms. Three of the walls were painted a warm rust color, and the fourth was a floor-to-ceiling blackboard. The board was covered in colorful writing and schematics. It was clearly an open invitation to anyone who entered to write down their ideas for all to see. The room was decorated with several intriguing pictures and an assortment of beautiful plants.

Sara sat behind a solid oak desk. Behind her was a huge oak-framed wall-hanging, which featured a rust-on-black statement. As Sara stood to greet him, Joe read the words:

> **ICE is a dynamic system for creating business wealth. It allows for the identification of a company's values and the feelings those values induce in one's stakeholders.**

Joe extended his hand across her desk and Sara grasped it warmly. "I'm Joe Tanner. Nice to meet you, Sara." Sara was dressed like a business professional. Joe decided immediately that he liked this confident young woman.

"Nice to meet you, Joe." Sara flicked her head toward the wall-hanging behind her. "You like the message?"

"It's why I'm here."

"So Wally tells me." She moved out from behind the desk. "Why don't we sit over here?" she suggested, indicating the cluster of luxurious, leather captains' chairs opposite her desk and facing the giant blackboard.

As Joe and Wally seated themselves, Sara moved to the blackboard. "Wally, have you explained my role in the company to Joe?"

"He only knows your title."

"My official one, or the one that really describes what I do?"

Wally laughed. "The official one." He turned to Joe. "Sara's known around here as the ICE Queen."

Sara smiled. "Nice, huh? I love it, but it's not a title that works real well on a business card."

"No, I wouldn't think so," replied Joe.

"But it does describe what I do. My role here is to run ICE sessions with every single department, and to address all the challenges we face on a daily basis."

"And Sara does a wonderful job. She understands the ICE formula better than anybody, and has a tremendous knack for extracting great ideas from our employee base," said Wally.

"Wally's being kind. The ICE system makes my job easy. Anybody who understands it and its power could do what I do.

"Let's start by explaining ICE in more detail. ICE — Internal Consulting Expertise — consists of a series of visual aids that, when used in sequence, can be applied to any part of your business. It can be used to address issues as complex as new product or service development, or issues as internally focused as your business processes. The foundation of ICE is the Value/Feeling equation in every company. We need to find yours, Joe. Once we've done that, we'll have taken a big step toward saving Tanner Enterprises."

"Where do we start?"

"With the ICE Value/Feeling concept maps." Sara touched a panel on the wall nearest her, and the image on the framed picture behind her desk changed.

Joe hadn't realized that the print behind Sara's desk was actually a high-resolution computer-generated image. "That's pretty impressive."

Sara smiled. "It's my favorite toy."

Sara stepped over to the new image. As she did, Joe examined it closely.

ICE VALUE/FEELING CONCEPT MAPS	
Map 1: Attractive Value/ Feeling Concepts	**Map 2: Value/Feeling Opportunity Gap**
the company follows through on its positive values, the stakeholder is happy	the company believes it is delivering on its positive values, but isn't quite giving the stakeholder what they really want
Best case scenario	*Room for overachievement*
Map 3: Repulsive Value/Feeling Concepts	**Map 4: Strategic Avoidance Zone**
the company promises to deliver on its positive values, but doesn't deliver at all	the company has poor values, ignores what the stakeholder really wants
Company not delivering	*Company in trouble*

Current gains come from map 1. Future gains come from maps 1 and 2. Feelings in map 3 should be addressed immediately. Avoid map 4.

Sara let Joe absorb the slide's meaning for a few moments before continuing. "Let me first explain what's meant by the term stakeholders. In this context, a stakeholder can be anybody who has a hand in your business. A stakeholder can be a customer, a supplier, an employee, an internal client, such as a PC user served by your information technology department, or even a shareholder."

"How about the marketplace in general?" asked Joe.

"That works, too. The ICE Value/Feeling model can be applied broadly."

"Can you elaborate on the four concept maps?"

"Oh, absolutely. You'll need to understand the maps

in depth to fully capitalize on ICE. Basically, map 1 is the ideal situation: you're giving your stakeholders exactly what they want. In map 2, you're still doing a good job, but you still have some room to find out what the stakeholders *really* want. In map 3, your company promises to deliver on its values and doesn't, instilling negative feelings in your stakeholders. Companies in a map 4 scenario are really in trouble. They ignore what the stakeholders want and don't have a clearly defined set of positive values."

Wally had a suggestion. "Sara, I sometimes find the Value/Feeling concept maps a little easier to understand when they're explained in the context of a real situation. Could you describe them using the customer growth strategies that we developed using ICE?"

"Good idea."

Wally turned to face his friend. "You'll like this one, Joe, and I think you'll be able to apply it at Tanner quickly, since you've indicated that achieving sustained growth is probably your greatest challenge. Also, you'll be able to relate directly to some of the outcomes from the ICE Value/Feeling process. Like Adrienne's reception-area program, for example."

"Lay it on me," replied Joe, enthusiastically.

Sustained
Revenue Growth

*A*fter a few cups of coffee, Joe, Sara, and Wally were ready to continue going over the various ICE concepts. Joe was taking in a lot of information in a short time, but he was beginning to understand why Wally was so confident in ICE.

Sara touched the panel and again the wall image changed. Joe read the new slide.

**ATTRACTIVE VALUE/FEELING
CONCEPT DEVELOPMENT**

What are the values and feelings that the company successfully creates and services for the customer?

VALUES   **FEELINGS**

_____   _____

_____   _____

_____   _____

_____   _____

_____   _____

_____   _____

_____   _____

"The visual aids I'm going to take you through, Joe, are used in every ICE session. The outcomes they generate are always different depending, of course, on the stakeholders."

Wally added, "What I like about the visual aids is that the outcomes are different even if the stakeholders remain the same."

"How so?"

Sara responded, "Because the business circumstances will have changed. The answer to a question asked three months ago may be very different when asked today."

"So, ICE accommodates change."

"That's right, Joe. ICE is a forever program, not a fad. It will always be relevant."

"When Sara took us through this, Joe, there were fifteen people in the room."

"And that was just one of the sessions. I covered a total of seventy-five employees who, collectively, represented every function and every level within the company. A smart company learns that Internal Consulting Expertise can come from anywhere in the company. The best ideas don't necessarily come from the top of the organization."

Joe glanced at the slide again. "Where do you start?"

"With the identification of the company's attractive values, and the determination of the feelings that living up to these values will create, we figure out what the values and feelings are for map 1," replied Sara. "After a fair amount of discussion, here's how we defined our

---

ATTRACTIVE VALUE/FEELING
CONCEPT DEVELOPMENT

What are the values to which the company subscribes and the related feelings our stakeholders have?

VALUES	FEELINGS
Stakeholder first	Important
Listen before you speak	Respected
Promises are commitments	Trust
Underpromise – overdeliver	Value
Poor quality is not an option	Reliability
One team	Consistent
Proactive, not reactive	Progressive
Celebrate success; learn from failure	Fun; empathy

---

attractive Value/Feeling proposition." Sara touched the panel and the slide changed.

Joe reviewed the slide carefully. "That is a pretty impressive set of values."

"They're religion at Walden Chase, Joe," said Wally. "And by operating according to our values, we are generating the kinds of feelings among our stakeholders we believed living to these values would create."

Joe examined the feelings associated with each value and tried to relate to them as a consumer might. "I can see that, Wally. If a company or an individual with whom I deal lived according to these values, these are the kinds of feelings I would have toward that company or person."

"That's what makes ICE so unique. It works on every level, and with any stakeholder."

Wally glanced at his watch. "Joe, I have to meet a colleague of mine for a quick lunch."

"Oh, of course."

As Wally departed, Sara asked, "It's almost noon. Are you hungry, Joe?"

Joe looked at his watch. "Wow. I can't believe I've been here this long. And, since you're asking, I am a little hungry. I was in a rush this morning, so I skipped breakfast."

"Breakfast is your fuel for the day."

"ICE?"

"No, mom." Sara chuckled. "It was probably the same at your house, too."

Joe smiled. Despite his problems, he hadn't felt this good in a long, long time. "It was. And you're right. I'll start eating better . . . mom."

Sara called to arrange for some food and then continued. "Let's talk about the Value/Feeling concept map 2, which helps us identify the Value/Feeling opportunity gap."

"Great."

"The premise behind this concept map is that there are feelings that stakeholders desire but aren't experiencing because a company is not executing its values in a way that stimulates the right feelings. Is that clear?"

"I think so." Joe didn't sound convinced.

Sara looked over Joe's shoulder and saw one of her associates standing in the doorway. The young man was delivering lunch. Sara smiled and politely signaled for him to wait. "Okay. One of our values is 'stakeholder first,' right?"

"Right."

"And the primary feeling we strive to create through application of this value is?"

"A feeling of importance."

"Exactly. Now, let's say we believed that one of our stakeholders, you for example, needed to feel not just important but special, too."

"Okay."

"Did the treatment you received today when you arrived make you feel special?"

Joe thought about how Adrienne had treated him when he first arrived. He recalled seeing his image digitally displayed beside two other individuals who had 9 A.M. appointments. "I can't say the greeting made me feel like I was receiving special treatment. It was great treatment, don't get me wrong, but no, it didn't make me feel special."

Sara waved over the lunch-toting associate. "Joe, meet Rob, one of our newest employees. Rob was kind enough to bring us our lunch." Rob set the tray down and the two men shook hands. After Rob left, Sara said, "Check out your lunch."

Joe looked puzzled, but did as asked. When he lifted the stainless steel lid covering his meal, his jaw dropped in amazement. "My . . . Wow! Where did you get this?"

"This" was a Big Ben's smoked meat sandwich. The only place in the world to buy a Big Ben's sandwich was at

Ben's, the famous Manhattan restaurant, which was three time zones away. This sandwich was Joe's favorite meal. He made a point of going to Big Ben's every time he visited New York. He hadn't been there for over three months.

"You once told Wally how much you loved these sandwiches."

"I remember," said Joe with a grin. "I think I told him that if I ever ended up on death row, this would be my last meal."

"Wally remembered that, so he made arrangements to have a fellow from our New York office, who was coming here today, pick up a sandwich on his way to the airport. Apparently Ben's is open early. I'm afraid we had to reheat it, though."

"That doesn't matter. They're wonderful even when they're cold." Joe took a huge bite of the smoked meat sandwich. "Oh, man, this is good!"

"How does having us bring you that sandwich make you feel, Joe?"

Joe looked up from his plate. Only one word came to mind. "Special. It makes me feel special. This is another ICE initiative, isn't it?"

"A somewhat dramatic version of it, but yes. It's typical of the kinds of initiatives that are derived from our Value/Feeling map 2 sessions." Sara stood and moved to the control panel. "This question serves as a catalyst for the process."

Joe read the question. "In many instances that might be a very hard question to answer."

ATTRACTIVE VALUE/FEELING
OPPORTUNITY DEVELOPMENT

What are the feelings that the stakeholder really wants but that the application of our values does not fully deliver?

VALUES	FEELINGS
Stakeholder first	_____
Listen before you speak	_____
Promises are commitments	_____
Underpromise – overdeliver	_____
Poor quality is not an option	_____
One team	_____
Proactive, not reactive	_____
Celebrate success; learn from failure	_____

"You're right, but why do you think that is?"

"It implies that you really know your stakeholder well. I can say with some assurance, for example, that my customers as stakeholders want to feel important. But can I say that they, as a group, need or want to feel special? I don't think so."

"How would you determine that?" Sara asked.

"I'd have to look at each customer on an individual basis."

Sara smiled. "You're right. And you've also just discovered the key to sustaining revenue growth with ICE. By applying the Value/Feeling map 2 process to each of your key customers, you will identify the feelings that they really want to have, and that you are not delivering."

Joe recalled the Value/Feeling Concept Map. "That's why map 2 helps define opportunities for future growth."

"Exactly. If application of your values creates those desired feelings in your customer, and if your competitors are not creating those same feelings, then you will have gained a competitive advantage," said Sara.

"I understand. But is there usually a feeling that a customer wants but that he's not getting associated with every value?"

"Not necessarily. In many cases it's as simple as finding the one feeling that the stakeholder really wants but is not getting. Let me give you an example." Sara went to her desk and tapped a few keys on the PC. The image behind her changed. "Here's a Value/Feeling map 2 we did for one of our key customers.

"As you can see, the feelings this customer wanted matched exactly with what we believed we were delivering to him, with one exception."

ATTRACTIVE VALUE/FEELING CONCEPT DEVELOPMENT

What are the feelings that the stakeholder really wants but that the application of our values does not fully deliver?

VALUES	FEELINGS
Stakeholder first	*Important*
Listen before you speak	*Respected*
Promises are commitments	*Trust*
Underpromise – overdeliver	*Value*
Poor quality is not an option	*Reliability*
One team	*Consistent*
Proactive, not reactive	***Visionary***
Celebrate success; learn from failure	*Fun; empathy*

Joe noted the word in bold — **Visionary.**

"Right. This particular client didn't just want to feel progressive, which was the feeling we were inspiring by living to our values. He needed to feel like a visionary within his industry. Once we discovered that, through ICE, we posed this question." Sara touched the wall panel and a new question appeared.

What can be done to inspire the kinds of feelings desired by our stakeholders?

"And through the answers developed by our ICE team we were able to develop a series of tactics that made our stakeholder — our customer — feel like a visionary."

"What kinds of tactics did you use in his case?"

"There were lots of them. For example, we nominated our customer and his company for a National Innovation award sponsored by his industry association. He didn't win, but the nomination spawned a series of speaking engagements for our customer that dramatically raised his personal profile as a visionary within his industry."

"And your tactics paid off?"

"We have captured 100 percent of his available business. And we've picked up a number of new deals that we might not otherwise have won, strictly due to referrals from our customer."

"That's pretty impressive," said Joe.

"It is. More importantly, it wasn't hard. It was simply a matter of applying a little ICE."

Wally walked back into the office. "So, how are you two making out?"

"Just great, Wally. I think I'm really getting a grasp of what ICE is all about."

"This is just the starting point, Joe. Now the fun really begins," said Sara. "Remember map 1? All we've done so far is to define what it is the stakeholder really wants and what feelings will be created if we deliver on those 'wants.' The next stage in the ICE process, map 3, looks at what the customer really does *not* want. This is the Repulsive Value/Feeling development exercise, in which we define what happens when a company and its people don't operate according to its values."

"This is where the process gets painful, right?"

Wally laughed. "The first time we went through this, it was brutal. Now, it's not so bad because our Values/Feelings are so in-bred that we instinctively avoid a lot of the repulsive feelings we once brought out in our stakeholders."

Sara touched the slide progression panel. "This image reflects the outcome of one of our first sessions. In this example, our customers were identified as our stakeholders. As part of the ICE process, we asked ourselves how our customers feel when we don't operate according to our values."

Joe looked at the slide and grinned. "I see you've edited out the profanity."

REPULSIVE VALUE/FEELING
CONCEPT DEVELOPMENT

What are our stakeholders' feelings when the company and its employees do not operate according to its values?

VALUES	FEELINGS
Stakeholder first	Neglected
Listen before you speak	Insulted
Promises are commitments	Disappointed
Underpromise – overdeliver	Distrustful
Poor quality is not an option	Angry
One team	Confused
Proactive, not reactive	Frustrated
Celebrate success; learn from failure	Bored

"Yeah, the X-rated version didn't get past our in-bred 'Poor quality is not an option' value," Sara replied with a chuckle.

Joe smiled at Sara, then focused again on the slide. "You know, I bet Tanner is generating every negative feeling you've listed among our many stakeholders."

"Most organizations do, Joe. And many organizations fail because they do," replied Wally. "About three years ago, I introduced ICE to a colleague of my brother's. His company had fallen on hard times and my brother felt it really needed ICE. They embraced the system, in theory, and went through the Value/Feeling development process, but they never really addressed the negative feelings they were creating with their stakeholders. The company went into receivership about a year ago. I'm convinced that it could have survived had they put the necessary plans of action into place and carried them out."

"Which takes us to the next stage in the process, Joe, where we start to develop the action plans necessary to turn these negative feelings into positive ones. This is where ICE really starts to deliver immediate and lasting value."

"Can you give me an example?"

"Of course. When this negative Value/Feeling list was developed with our Internal Consulting Experts, we created a list of ways in which we were causing these repulsive feelings."

"We're back to Adrienne," said Wally.

"That's right, Wally," replied Sara. "Adrienne was a member of our ICE team, and what we learned from her was really enlightening."

"How so?" asked Joe.

"Well, we started at the top of this list, naturally, and we tried to identify ways in which we caused repulsive feelings in our customers. Remember, the stakeholder in this exercise was our customers."

"Right."

"So, in trying to cite examples of how we had created negative feelings, Adrienne explained how we turned off many of our customers by keeping them hanging around the lobby past their agreed-upon appointment time because we weren't ready to receive them!"

Wally shook his head. "Can you imagine?"

"The more ICE we received from Adrienne, the clearer

the picture became. In fact, we had lost the Bradley Inc. account some three months earlier, and it wasn't until Adrienne explained how neglected and unimportant we made our customer feel that we understood why. Adrienne didn't know who Mr. Bradley was, or how important his account was to Walden Chase. All she knew was that, after waiting twenty minutes to see our VP of sales, Mr. Bradley approached her and said, 'When Ben finally decides I'm worth seeing, tell him I'm tired of waiting. It's like this every time I come here. Funny, when he comes to see me I show him in right away. Amazing, isn't it? Makes you wonder who the customer really is.' We lost the Bradley account to our major competitor less than a week later. Until we received a little ICE from Adrienne, we had thought we'd lost Bradley's business due to price."

"Our behavior evoked feelings of neglect in Mr. Bradley," added Wally. "We made him feel unimportant. Adrienne's ICE showed us that. As a result, we implemented our promptness strategy."

Joe recalled Adrienne's words from earlier that day: *Promptness is a way of life at Walden Chase.* "So, your entire reception area approach originated with Adrienne's Internal Consulting Expertise?"

"Right," answered Sara. She touched the control panel and a new slide appeared.

How will the company address repulsive feelings so that the stakeholder becomes attracted again to the company?

"Adrienne's ICE served as the catalyst for the development of an entire 'customer first' strategy. One of the tactics called for redesign of our reception service. Adrienne developed the tactical plan. It included everything, including the reception area layout."

"The 'tag' part as well?" asked Joe.

"The 'tag' part, too," said Sara.

"How did the reception you received from us today make you feel?" asked Wally.

Joe replied, "It was great. I really felt important."

"And customers buy from a company based on how it and its people make you feel."

Joe thought about what his squash buddy had just said. Wally was absolutely right. How one's customer *felt* about you and your company was more important than anything they *thought*. The Value/Feeling concept was very real, and entirely applicable to Tanner Enterprises.

Sara continued, "Once we had defined all of the strategies and tactics that would address the repulsive feelings we had been creating by not adhering to our values, we then used ICE to put a little FIRE into the company."

"FIRE? Don't tell me there's another program I've never heard of."

"It's not a program. It's an acronym that stands for Fresh Ideas Re-energize Enterprises. It's designed to generate ideas beyond the obvious ones," replied Sara.

Wally nodded his head. "Actually, Adrienne's image-scanning initiative was the product of a FIRE session."

"How does FIRE work?"

"FIRE is pretty simple," replied Sara. "Once an ICE team has defined the strategies and tactics necessary to correct repulsive feelings, the team is put through a FIRE session designed to stretch the limits of their thinking. FIRE asks the ICE team members to answer this simple question." Sara touched the wall control and a new slide appeared.

What new initiatives could be introduced to make the stakeholder feel even more important?

Sara continued, "It's a really an exercise that says, okay, you've thought of all the strategies and tactics you can. Now, push yourselves beyond that. Use some off-the-wall thinking."

"And the image-scanning idea derived from a FIRE session?"

"That and myriad other great ideas we've adopted at Walden Chase," replied Wally. "It always seems that the best ideas come from the FIRE sessions because by that time the obvious stuff has been talked over."

"Interesting," said Joe. "And is FIRE always used in conjunction with ICE?"

"Always. It's part of the system. Since we're always exploring ways of correcting repulsive feelings and creating positive feelings, it's simply a matter of putting the feeling you're discussing into the question," replied Sara.

Joe examined the slide again. "I see. So if I were trying to probe for fresh ideas on how to, say, create feelings that would make a particular stakeholder feel more respected, I'd simply insert the word 'respect' in the sentence in place of 'important.'"

Sara nodded. "That's right. A pretty simple way of tapping into breakthrough thinking, isn't it?"

"It sure is. I'm trying to recall the matrix slide you showed me — the one with the ICE Value/Feeling concept maps."

Sara touched the control panel. "Let me redisplay it for you."

ICE VALUE/FEELING CONCEPT MAPS	
Map 1: Attractive Value/ Feeling Concepts	*Map 2: Value/Feeling Opportunity Gap*
the company follows through on its positive values, the stakeholder is happy	the company believes it is delivering on its positive values, but isn't quite giving the stakeholder what they really want
Best case scenario	*Room for overachievement*
Map 3: Repulsive Value/Feeling Concepts	*Map 4: Strategic Avoidance Zone*
the company promises to deliver on its positive values, but doesn't deliver at all	the company has poor values, ignores what the stakeholder really wants
Company not delivering	*Company in trouble*

Current gains come from map 1. Future gains come from maps 1 and 2. Feelings in map 3 should be addressed immediately. Avoid map 4.

Joe re-examined the slide. "Can you explain how ICE is applied in map 4?"

Before Sara could reply, Wally said, "Joe, if you don't mind, I'm going to leave you in Sara's hands for a while."

"Certainly."

"I'll walk Joe through map 4, Wally. It'll take about half an hour."

Wally stood. "That'll give me the time I need to make a few calls. I call ten customers every day. It's a —"

Joe interrupted. "Let me guess. A Walden Chase principle."

Wally smiled. "Compliments of . . ."

"ICE."

Wally laughed. "The guy's a quick study. I'll be back in thirty minutes."

Sara touched the slide control panel and a new image appeared. "Let's talk about the final Value/Feeling Concept Map, map 4." A new image appeared.

As Joe scanned the image, Sara said, "I call this the 'dirty laundry' session. This is where you really start to discover the values that are being demonstrated by your company and that are destroying your business."

"I've always thought of values as innately positive."

"That's how they're most commonly viewed, but a value doesn't have to be positive. Let's say, for example, my primary value was 'anything for money.' That could lead to some pretty negative behavior."

Joe chuckled. "Robbing banks and dealing crack as key tactics in my anything-for-money strategy. I see

---

STRATEGIC AVOIDANCE
VALUE/FEELING CONCEPT DEVELOPMENT

What are the values that the company must avoid to prevent instilling negative feelings in its stakeholders that will erode the company's market position and might destroy the company?

VALUES   **FEELINGS**

_____   _____

_____   _____

_____   _____

_____   _____

_____   _____

_____   _____

_____   _____

---

what you mean." Sara smiled and Joe continued. "Are you comfortable sharing the results of Walden Chase's Strategic Avoidance Value/Feeling exercise?"

Sara laughed. "Do I want to show you our dirty laundry? Sure. We had a lot of it, of course, depending on which stakeholder we were discussing." Sara touched the wall control. "We've been talking about the customer as stakeholder, so let's continue in that vein. ICE told us we needed to avoid these values, and helped us figure out the feelings that we were creating when we displayed these values to our customers."

STRATEGIC AVOIDANCE
VALUE/FEELING CONCEPT DEVELOPMENT

What are the values that the company must avoid to prevent instilling negative feelings in its stakeholders that will erode the company's market position and might destroy the company?

VALUES	FEELINGS
"Me" first	Unimportant
Speak, don't listen	Disrespected
Promises are meaningless	Betrayed
Overpromise – Underdeliver	Manipulated
Quantity, not quality	Used
Every one for themselves	Confused
Reactive, not proactive	Ignored
Ignore success; punish failure	Bored; disappointed

Joe reviewed the slide. "Interesting. The 'me-first' value. Is that at the individual or corporate level, as in company first?"

"It could be either or both. When people put their personal interests or those of their company ahead of the stakeholder's, the feelings that are brought out are always the same."

"A feeling of unimportance."

"Exactly." Sara changed the slide.

Where are we displaying Strategic Avoidance Values/Feelings and what kinds of outcomes are we observing among our stakeholders?

"In responding to this question, which was posed in one ICE session, we identified a remarkable example of where this was occurring in our regional sales offices. Our customer surveys were telling us that customers were increasingly dissatisfied with the service they were receiving from their respective account teams. Comments such as, 'We don't see enough of them,' 'They're inaccessible,' and 'They're delivering little or no value' were common. What ICE revealed was that over the years we had become internally focused. Many of our regional staff spent as much time dealing with internal-reporting issues as they did with their customers. Through ICE we uncovered several things that were causing this phenomenon."

"Whats kind of things?"

"The most amusing one involved Wally. Adam Cain is our vice-president responsible for the regional offices. Adam reports to Wally. Seems like, oh, about three years ago, Wally told Adam that he'd like a weekly report on some of the key initiatives that were being worked on by the various regions. So, one thing led to another and the next thing you know Adam and his regional counterparts — all ninety-seven of them — were producing a comprehensive weekly highlights report. These reports were consolidated at head office and we had — get this — a full-time employee reviewing all of the monthly input and collapsing it into one two-page report for Wally. Of course, only the largest deals were included."

Joe looked a little sheepish. Sara asked, "What's up?"

"Well, this is almost embarrassing. I get the same kind of report every week," Joe replied. "I think I'm going to be sick."

Sara laughed. "It gets worse. Anyway, we figured out how much it was costing the company to produce this little highlight report, and we estimated that we were engaging the equivalent of ten to twelve people across several regions to publish it."

"Ouch! Considering what it costs to employ someone today, that would represent a loaded cost of over a million dollars a year."

"Exactly. And you know what?"

"What?"

"Wally hardly ever had time to read the report! Do you read *your* report?"

Joe grimaced. "Once in a while."

"When ICE was further applied to this particular situation, we realized that this was just one of the internal reporting requirements we were placing on the regional sales people, all in the interest of knowing what was going on in the business."

"But not in the interest of *growing* the business."

"Precisely."

"So what did you do?"

"ICE solved it. Once the Strategic Avoidance Value/ Feeling map was completed, we then proceeded to the next step in the process by asking the ICE team this." Sara touched the control panel and a new image appeared on the screen.

What can we do to eliminate the
application of strategic avoidance values
and prevent the creation of corresponding
negative feelings in our stakeholders?

"So answering this question leads to the development of the tactics necessary to eliminate the negative values a company or its people might be displaying?"

"Right."

"What happened in this particular case?"

"With the regions? Oh, we assessed the value of every single report that was being generated for internal information or communication purposes. We killed two-thirds of them. And of the ones that remained, we turned half of them into voice reports."

"Voice reports?"

"One of our ICE sessions led to our using some of the spare capacity on our integrated voice response system to establish a regional reporting application."

Joe smiled. They used IVR at Tanner Enterprises. It was the technology that enabled automated answering and routing of calls with the familiar 'press one for subject A, press two for subject B' type of menu. "How do the voice reports work?"

"It's pretty simple. The regional managers simply call in once a week and 'drop' a voice message into the IVR system. Wally, or anybody else for that matter, can simply call in and retrieve the messages at their discretion. The system allows for searching, so the people seeking the information can request a report from a particular office, or ask for the voice reports that mention a particular product or customer."

"That's amazing."

"What's more amazing is that we had no idea our system could do this. We learned of its capabilities from a young computer whiz-kid who participated in an ICE session."

"You had an expert in-house?"

"That's right. An Internal Consulting Expert we would never have accessed had we not applied ICE."

"Were you able to quantify the results of this particular program?"

"Yes. Our customer surveys have confirmed that our customer satisfaction rate has risen dramatically. Also, our sales people are much happier, and regional revenues are up significantly."

"Wow!"

"And it was so simple. All we had to do was to identify where we were displaying negative values, understand the kind of feelings these values were creating, then develop the tactics necessary to avoid them."

"How's it going?" Joe looked up to see Wally standing in the doorway.

"It's going great, Wally. Sara's doing a wonderful job in introducing me to ICE."

"I think his favorite part was the sandwich."

They all laughed. Joe said, "She's right. That was amazing. ICE and a Big Ben. What more could a man ask for?"

"Joe, I could walk you through the rest of the customer-as-stakeholder exercise we conducted if you think it would be worthwhile," volunteered Sara.

"Or if you think the concept of ICE is clear enough," added Wally, "perhaps we could redirect our energies toward applying ICE within Tanner Enterprises. What do you think?"

"I think I'm grasping the power of ICE, Wally, and it's clear that it's had a big impact on Walden Chase. I'm anxious to apply the principles at Tanner, so maybe we should focus on that."

"That makes sense. By the way, Joe, Sara is your personal ICE resource until you have time to develop your own. She'll be with you every step of the way."

"Wally, I don't know how to thank you."

"Save Tanner Enterprises. I can't think of a better thank you than that."

5

Saving Tanner Enterprises

*J*oe's mind was racing as he left the Walden Chase parking lot. The ICE process was simple, but brilliant, and it had clearly made a big difference at Walden Chase. But they had been applying ICE for years. Joe was convinced that ICE could help improve Tanner Enterprise's situation. He just wasn't certain that ICE could make a difference in the 24 hours he had left to formulate a survival plan for his company. He'd find out, though. Project ICE was about to begin.

Joe settled into the flow of traffic, then placed a cellular call to his office. Rachel, his assistant, answered, and at Joe's request she directed his call to their voice-mail service. Joe selected broadcast, then activated the hands-free feature on his phone. "Hi, gang. It's Joe at around 4:15, and this is a broadcast message to my direct reports. I know that each of you are working feverishly in preparation for tomorrow's 5 o'clock meeting. There's been a change of plans, however, and I want to now communicate what will take place tomorrow morning at 7 sharp. Each of you is going to participate in a four-hour training session on ICE. You'll find out tomorrow what ICE is, but trust me — you'll be impressed. Afterwards, each of you will convene meetings with fifteen key people within your respective departments. Select those people this evening, and please ensure that you have represented every level in your organization, and as many functions as possible. I want new employees, long-term employees, senior managers and entry-level workers. This is very important, so please try and get the right mix. Also, pick individuals who are well regarded in the company. We need our best thinkers in these sessions.

"Guys, I know this request seems like a peculiar one given our grave situation, but it's likely not much more peculiar than the directive that I communicated this morning, to fire all our consultants. These requests are related, and you'll understand how tomorrow. Again, please trust me. I truly believe we're doing what's necessary to save Tanner Enterprises. See you in the morning. Thanks."

Joe released the call and let out a big sigh. Tomorrow was going to be one amazing day.

The atmosphere in the meeting room was electric. For the past three hours Sara Daly had been taking the members of Joe's executive team through the ICE process, and with every new example she introduced, the energy level in the room grew. Joe could feel it. Chelsea Bain,

Tanner's VP of strategic planning, was clearly the most energized. At the mid-morning break Joe had asked her what she thought, and she had replied with one word: "Breakthrough." Her smile said the rest.

Joe watched as Sara Daly took the team through the last phase of the training exercise. He glanced at his watch. It was almost noon. Crunch time. He was now mere hours from finding out whether or not his big gamble on ICE was about to pay off.

". . . so, ladies and gentlemen. That, in a nutshell, is ICE."

The team applauded Sara for her efforts and she was clearly appreciative. "Gee, that's the first time I've ever received applause for a training session. I'm over-whelmed. Thank you so much!"

Joe rose from his chair. "Thank *you*, Sara. And, believe me, the applause is well deserved." He moved to the front of the room to stand beside her. Once there, he turned to face his executive team. "Well, guys, this is it. Kent and I are meeting with our financiers tomorrow at 10 A.M. Quite frankly, just two days ago my expectation was that at that meeting Tanner Enterprises would be placed in receivership. I know for a fact that we have lost the confidence of the entire financial community and, despite what I may have hoped for, I couldn't right-fully expect our bankers to support our business any longer. Kent agrees with me." Joe paused before contin-uing. "Now, I think, we have hope. We need to engage ICE and we need to do it now. I know each of you has arranged for ICE sessions related to your specific areas of responsibility. The outcome of these sessions is crucial. I need each of you to take your best shot at defining the strategic direction for your units and the tactical plans that put those strategies into action. You will have to have your plans in place by 8 P.M." Joe smiled and said, "Chelsea, I hope you brought your toothbrush. You, Kent, and I may be in for an all-nighter."

"Whatever it takes, Joe."

Sara, still standing at Joe's side, touched him gently on the shoulder to get his attention. "Joe, you mean you, Chelsea, Kent, *and me.*"

"Sara, I can't possibly ask this of you —"

"Are you kidding? This is the ultimate test for ICE. Just try and keep me away!"

"We could use your help. Thank you."

"You're welcome. And by the way, Wally has one more surprise in store for you and your team."

"Really?"

"Really." Sara glanced at her watch and moved to the door of the conference room. She opened it and greeted a number of people standing outside the door. She invited them into the room and, as they entered, Sara declared, "Ladies and gentlemen, I'd like to introduce you to several members of Walden Chase's ICE squad. These men and women are ICE specialists in various disciplines. They're here to help you in your afternoon sessions. They aren't going to run your sessions for you, but they will help you get past any rough spots along the way." Sara looked directly at Joe. "Given the time frame you're dealing with, we thought it might help a little if we brought in some reinforcements."

"Sara, this is wonderful. Thank you so much." Joe turned his attention to the ICE facilitators. "And, thank you."

The ICE squad introduced themselves and informed everyone about their areas of expertise. Sara had thought of everything. There was an ICE facilitator available to each of Joe's executive team — one each for sales, marketing, information technology, finance and administration, operations, and human resources. And, of course, there was Sara, who quickly aligned herself with Tanner's VP of strategic planning, Chelsea Bain.

As the newcomers circulated throughout the room, shaking hands with the members of his team, Joe took a deep breath. The most challenging twenty-four hours of his life were about to begin.

Optimizing Information Technology

Sara Daly and Chelsea Bain spent an hour after the morning session laying out the format for the presentation that would be delivered by Joe and Tanner's CFO, Kent Waters, to the various financiers who were keeping Tanner Enterprises afloat. The presentation format was pretty simple: It arrayed the key strategies developed in each of the departmental ICE sessions, and outlined the key tactics that Tanner would initiate to deliver on these strategies. In each case, the financial impact on the company was fully explained.

Everyone at Tanner hoped — and Sara firmly believed — that the ICE sessions would help them portray a company with a solid strategy, one that suggested a bright financial future.

Sara had decided that Tanner had an excellent resource in Chelsea Bain. She had picked up the ICE formula rapidly, and would certainly be able to keep ICE going at Tanner Enterprises long after Sara and her team had departed. Tanner was about to unleash its very own "ICE Queen."

"What do you think about the presentation format?" asked Chelsea.

"I love it. You've taken a nice, simple approach aimed at the right level."

"I don't think these guys are going to want to get into the nitty-gritty."

"I agree. Let's keep our perspective at fifty-thousand feet. If they want more detail beyond that, we can provide it later. In fact, if they do request more information, that will be a good sign."

"No quick decisions, in other words."

"Exactly."

Chelsea saved the file and backed it up. "Now what?"

"We start to make the rounds to see how the ICE sessions are going and to see if they need any help."

"Okay."

"Where would you like to start?" Sara asked.

Chelsea thought for a moment before replying. "How about with our information technology team? They certainly have some huge challenges."

Sara and Chelsea entered the conference room. It was immediately apparent to them that the team assembled to address Tanner's information technology issues was completely engaged in the ICE process. Sara's and Chelsea's arrival was barely acknowledged. Chelsea glanced at the screen at the front of the room to see the now-familiar Value/Feeling concept map.

ICE VALUE/FEELING CONCEPT MAPS	
Map 1: Attractive Value/ Feeling Concepts	**Map 2: Value/Feeling Opportunity Gap**
the company follows through on its positive values, the stakeholder is happy	the company believes it is delivering on its positive values, but isn't quite giving the stakeholder what they really want
Best case scenario	*Room for overachievement*
Map 3: Repulsive Value/Feeling Concepts	**Map 4: Strategic Avoidance Zone**
the company promises to deliver on its positive values, but doesn't deliver at all	the company has poor values, ignores what the stakeholder really wants
Company not delivering	*Company in trouble*

Current gains come from map 1. Future gains come from maps 1 and 2. Feelings in map 3 should be addressed immediately. Avoid map 4.

Tanner's VP of information technology, Jay Cameron, was at the front of the room with his new sidekick, Walden Chase ICE specialist Nancy Lee. The team was focused on the definition of the map 1 Values/Feelings for their team.

"So, just to reinforce the concepts that Nancy reviewed with us earlier," Jay said, "let's again look at the Value/Feeling concept maps." He paused for a moment to let the ICE team study the image. "Our exercise now is to define the values we need to subscribe to and, once we've done that, to define the feelings that living to these values will generate."

Nancy added, "Is everybody comfortable with who you've defined as your stakeholder?"

There were nods throughout the room. "Reg," asked Nancy, "Could you tell us what you think just to make sure we're all on the same wavelength?" Reg was a long-term employee who was responsible for Tanner's data networks.

"Glad to. Our stakeholders are primarily the employees of this company — the people who use information technology tools in their day-to-day jobs. We also have a secondary list of stakeholders, which I don't think we knew we had before this session — our trading partners." Reg looked in the direction of one of the junior engineers. "A little ICE from Katie helped us understand that."

"I agree. That was an eye-opener for me, too, Katie," added Jay. "It really broadens our definition of stakeholders."

Nancy continued, "And I think you'll find, as we move forward into the map 3 Value/Feeling development process, that this expansion of your stakeholder definition will afford you a number of opportunities that you didn't know were there before."

"That's what we're looking for," said Jay. He moved to the PC, which was plugged into the projection panel. "While we were discussing map 1, Nancy was busily keying in the outcome of our Value/Feeling development exercise."

A new image appeared on the screen.

ATTRACTIVE VALUE/FEELING
CONCEPT DEVELOPMENT

What are the values to which the company subscribes and the related feelings instilled in its stakeholders?

VALUES	FEELINGS
Stakeholders rule	Respected
IT enables the vision	Supported
Deliver what's promised	Trust
Underpromise – overdeliver	Value
Failure is not an option	Reliable
Leading edge	Strategic
IT as a strategic advantage	Competitive
Reward success	Appreciated

The room went silent for a moment as the team reviewed the results of their efforts. Jay broke the silence. "It's interesting to see how many of these values are similar to those of Walden Chase." Jay had reviewed the other company's values in the morning training session.

"That's quite common." Sara replied. "In fact, you'll find as you review the results of the various ICE sessions being run this afternoon that the Value/Feeling Maps will also be very similar."

"That makes sense," interjected Nancy. "There are really only a handful of values that can be subscribed to. And my guess is that the very best companies operate according to very similar values."

"You're right," replied Sara. "Before you move to the

next phase in your session, would you mind very much walking through some of the thinking that went into defining, say, your 'Information technology enables the vision' value?"

"Not at all. Bill, you felt pretty strongly about this value. Care to comment?"

"Sure."

"Before you do, Bill, can you tell me a little about yourself?" asked Sara.

"Oh, sure. I've been with Tanner Enterprises for about four years. I'm part of our tech-support team, which means that I help people overcome problems with their PCs."

"What are your hobbies?"

Jay thought Sara's question was peculiar, until Bill answered it. "I'm a computer geek," he said and a shy grin spread across his face. "I write a regular column for a friend of mine's web site, and I do a lot of weekend consulting for friends of my dad."

"What's your dad do?"

Bill blushed. "Um, he's the CEO at MicroLab." MicroLab was one of the area's biggest, and most successful, high-technology companies.

"I see you come by your talent naturally. What kind of consulting do you do for your dad's friends?"

"Mostly helping them set up and maintain their home-computing systems."

"And why do you feel that Tanner Enterprises should be living to an 'IT enables the vision' value?"

"Well, I'm probably stealing some of my Dad's ideas here —"

"That's okay, Bill. It's smart. Why re-invent the wheel? We should all try and learn from successful companies, and from successful people like your dad."

"I'll tell him you said that. Anyway, my dad always says that his department's role is to deploy technologies that will enable the delivery of the company's vision. He thinks that too many companies have IT departments that operate in silos."

"Meaning?"

"Meaning that some IT organizations live for technology and are allowed to operate independent of a company's vision, like they are in an entirely different organization. When this happens, the likelihood of the right technologies being developed by the company is greatly diminished. And without the right technology in today's world, visions can never become reality."

It was clear from Jay's expression that he couldn't believe the wealth of knowledge that this young man, buried deep in his organization, had. Sara had seen the look many times before. ICE was working.

"Thanks, Bill," said Sara. She turned to Chelsea. "How about we move along to one of the other sessions? Looks like these guys have things well in hand."

7

Selling
More Effectively

*B*en Riley, Tanner's vice-president of sales, had happily welcomed the expertise of Charlie Gifford, the ICE consultant from Walden Chase. When Sara and Chelsea entered the conference room, Charlie was speaking to the team.

"Let's re-visit the Values/Feelings we have defined for this department, which we believe are consistent with the values of the company." He placed the overhead on the projector.

After giving the group a minute to review the image, Charlie replaced it with a new one. "Let's start with our first Value/Feeling, 'Customer rules,' as the value that generates a feeling of importance in our customers, and think about it with map 2 in mind. What new initiative could be introduced to make our customers feel more important?"

After a few moments, Ben said, "We could try and spend more time with our customers, which might make them feel more important."

ATTRACTIVE VALUE/FEELING CONCEPT DEVELOPMENT

What are the values to which the sales department subscribes and the related feelings instilled in our customers?

VALUES	*FEELINGS*
Customer rules	*Important*
Listen and learn	*Respected*
Honesty always	*Trusting*
Sell what's needed, not what's saleable	*Fulfilled*
Single point of contact	*In control*
Proactive, not reactive	*Helped*
Celebrate success	*Appreciated*
Never say die	*Admired*

"Ben, as it is we're working sixty hours a week. We don't have any more time to see our customers," remarked Mary Powell, one of Tanner's top sales representatives.

"I guess you're right, Mary. I know the kind of hours you and your colleagues spend on the job." He addressed the entire team. "Any other suggestions?"

"You guys want to hear my cookie story?" offered Gloria Murphy. Gloria was a fairly new sales support employee Ben had not met before today.

"Go for it, Gloria," replied Mary. "It has to be better than Ben's 'work harder' suggestion." Ben smiled and turned red.

Gloria waited until the laughter stopped before continuing. "Well, I'm a Girl Guide leader . . ." she paused, nervously.

Mary sensed Gloria's anxiety. "Hey, if you're as good a Guide leader as you are at your job, those Guides must be the best in the country."

"Thanks, Mary. Each year, as you probably know, we sell cookies to raise money for the Guide program. We usually have about two weeks to sell the cookies, but due to some kind of a mix-up, we didn't receive our cookies until the final weekend before we had to turn in our money and any unsold cookies. Now I know this seems kind of trivial, but selling our cookies is important to us. The money from the cookie sales finances many of our programs during the year."

"So what did you do?" asked Ben.

"Well, I sat down with the Guides — all twenty-eight of them — and we talked about what we could do to sell the most cookies in the limited time we had left. One of the girls, a little sweetie named Diane who had sold more cookies than any other member of my troop the previous two years, said, 'Let's just sell the cookies to the people we know will buy them.' I wasn't quite sure what she meant so I asked her to explain. She said, 'I've been selling cookies in my neighborhood for a few years now, and I kind of know who buys the cookies and who doesn't. So, now I only go to the people who I'm pretty sure will buy from me — the grammas and grandpas houses and the places that have little kids. Also, I used to try and sell the cookies outside the grocery store, but the people were always too busy, so I didn't sell too many. Instead I went to the video store in our neighborhood, and they let me put a cookie display on the counter. Even when I wasn't there, I was selling cookies.'"

Gloria paused, but no one wanted to interrupt her, so she continued. "Anyway, I realized that what little Diane had done was two things: she had segmented her neighborhood into high potential and low potential customers, and then sold only to the high potential ones, and she had established an alternate sales channel. And, by the way, I'm not trying to sound like an expert here, but I took a marketing course in college, so I'm just trying to express what she did in business terms."

"No, this is intriguing. What happened next?" asked Ben.

"We took Diane's advice. We had each of the kids segment their own neighborhoods and call only on the high-potential houses. The results were phenomenal. Every one of our Guides started delivering sales volumes at a Diane-like level. And while they did that, I hit all the video stores in our community and convinced them to display our cookies. In the forty-eight hours left, we sold every single box of cookies we had."

"Gloria's on to something, Ben," said Mary. "We try and give equal time to all of our accounts — in fact, our call-plan program ensures that we do — but we are wasting our time on half of our calls. I know in my case there are customers who will likely never buy from us."

One of Mary's colleagues, a sales manager named Matt, chipped in. "Mary's right, Ben. I bet if we didn't have to call on every account as often as we do we could increase our revenues by upwards of five percent."

"Matt, if that's the case, why haven't you done it before?" asked Ben.

"Simple. Our compensation plan. Our commission payouts are factored against the percentage of customer satisfaction we achieve. When we conduct surveys for customer satisfaction, we include all of these dog accounts in the results. If we weren't calling on them regularly, we'd get killed on this measurement and our commission earnings would go in the toilet."

Mary added, "We make more money by calling on these guys even if we sell less."

Ben shook his head. "Wow. There is a huge opportunity here. If we can segment —"

"That'll be easy," interrupted Matt.

"And if we only measure customer satisfaction on our high priority accounts . . . " added Mary.

"We can do that," said Ben. "In fact, in a segmented approach like this, it's only common sense to measure this way."

"If we do, Ben, I'll guarantee an extra five percent growth over what we've planned for next year," volunteered Matt.

Ben smiled at Gloria. "You're a genius."

"Thanks, but what about the alternate channels?"

"Well, we already have alternate channels carrying our product lines," replied Ben.

"We do, but they aren't set up the way Diane set up hers," said Matt.

"What do you mean?"

"Our alternate channels often compete with our direct sales force, for one thing. In fact, three of the biggest deals we lost last year were won by one of *our own* alternate channels."

"Isn't that good for Tanner?" asked Ben.

"Maybe, maybe not. In two of those cases, our products were the only ones being considered. I guarantee we left money on the table. Even when we do win, our margins are very thin."

"I'm open for suggestions," offered Ben.

"May I say something?"

"Of course, Gloria."

"Well, it seems to me that what made Diane successful was that her alternate channel didn't compete with her direct sales efforts. Or if it did, it wasn't evident to the consumer. Also, the sales that her video store channel made were credited to her overall sales results. So, she was happy when her alternate channel made a sale. It doesn't sound like we have this kind of situation here."

"You're absolutely right, Gloria," agreed Matt. "Ben, we should reposition our alternate channels so that they are selling primarily where we are not. In fact, once we complete our market segmentation, we could give them exclusive access to all the accounts that we aren't going to be calling on. They probably have better relationships than we do with those customers, anyway."

Mary added, "Then we should ensure that whatever sales originate with the channels result in some kind of override commission payout for the sales people. It doesn't have to be big, just enough for us to see the channels as our allies and not as our enemies. If something like this were in place, I could even see giving these guys leads occasionally."

"The extra commissions paid could come from the additional margin on deals that the company would win by not competing with itself."

"You're right, Matt. This seems so simple. I don't know why I didn't see it myself," said Ben, incredulous.

Sara had remained quiet during the segmentation and alternate channel dialogue. She sensed in Ben's last remark a feeling of failure for not having led the team to the same conclusions that ICE just had.

"Ben, that's exactly why ICE is so important to a company," she said. "No individual can dream up every great idea. We've created a business culture in this country that suggests that the guys on top have to make every decision. ICE proves otherwise. Too often the senior executives are so busy running their jobs and dealing with the day-to-day issues within their areas of responsibility, that they don't have time to do the one thing they should be doing more than anything else."

"What's that?" asked Ben.

"Think." Sara paused before continuing. "When was the last time you actually had a few hours to yourself to think about the job and what needs to be done?"

"I can't remember," answered Ben.

"And you're likely in the same boat as every other executive in this company. That's what makes ICE so valuable. Not only does ICE give you time to think, it allows you access to the tremendous expertise already in your company. Did you ever, even for a minute, think that one of your sales support people would help you shape the direction of your department by showing you how to make your customers feel more important?"

Ben grinned sheepishly. "I wouldn't have even sought out her opinion in the past."

"And now?"

"Now?" Ben chuckled, "I don't think I'll make a move without Gloria — and ICE!"

More
Dynamic Marketing

*J*oe was also making the rounds of the various ICE sessions, observing the process and contributing as best he could. The marketing ICE team had just completed their Attractive Value/Feeling Concept map development, and were now starting to define map 3, their Repulsive Value/Feeling map. Bill Conrad, vice-president of marketing, was completely engaged in the process and was using something that Joe had not seen in him in quite a while: his sense of humor. The members of the team were responding accordingly and, despite the nature of the subject they were discussing, the room was filled with laughter — the same kind of laughter Joe had heard at Walden Chase. The sound was music to Joe's ears.

One of Bill's product managers, Elaine O'Reilly, had the floor, and she was using an example of negative Value/Feeling creation to illustrate a point.

"Bill, you're fooling yourself if you think we are living up to our 'Poor quality is not an option' value. Look at our ConneX software launch."

"What about it?"

"We released it a good three months before it was ready, simply because we'd publicly committed to doing so."

"It would have been a public relations disaster if we'd delayed that release."

"Instead, we angered a lot of our best customers. Isn't that right, Karen?" Karen was one of the client representatives who handled customer service calls.

"The bugs in the ConneX release caused a lot of problems, particularly for our customers in the financial sector."

Bill remembered the numerous complaints. A glitch in the software had caused a decimal point shift whenever the numbers six and seven appeared consecutively. "Yeah, that wasn't pleasant. We did fix the problem pretty quickly, though."

"Our recovery was great, Bill," said Elaine, "but we needlessly created a lot of anger among our customer base by launching ConneX too early. We weren't adhering to our 'quality' value, and it cost us."

"Elaine's right, Bill," added Joe. "And when I think about it, we ended up with a PR problem anyway."

"Yes, you're right," agreed Bill, sheepishly. "The industry trades slammed us."

"When are we planning to release Platinum?" asked Karen. Platinum was the code name for the next release of ConneX.

Bill looked at Joe. Each knew what the other was thinking. If ICE didn't come through, Tanner Enterprises may not be releasing anything ever again. "We're planning to release it in three weeks time, Karen, at the ComWorld show in Chicago," announced Bill.

"Why then?"

"Well, it's a great opportunity for product exposure."

"Is the software robust this time? And if it isn't, what kinds of feelings will our customers have if they buy Platinum before we've developed it to the level of quality they deserve?"

Bill was taken aback by Karen's question. She was, after all, just an entry-level service representative. Before replying, however, he glanced at the image that was projected on the wall, and his eyes settled on the "respect for the individual" value that they had earlier agreed was an important one to subscribe to at Tanner Enterprises. Just six short hours before, he might not have made time for somebody like Karen. Now, he realized, if he and Tanner were to succeed, he had to listen. The Karens of the company were the ones to save it. "Karen, you raise a good point. If we push to launch Platinum before it's really ready for our customers to use, we'll make them angry."

"And probably cause a lot of resentment among those who stayed with us while we fixed the bugs from the last release," added Elaine.

Joe joined Bill at the front of the room. "Isn't this where we ask ourselves what we can do to change these feelings?"

"You're right," said Bill. He removed the Repulsive

Value/Feeling Concept Development slide and replaced it with the next slide in the ICE process.

How will the company correct the repulsive feelings so that the stakeholder becomes attracted to the company?

As Bill placed the slide on the projector, the conference room door opened and Sara and Chelsea entered. Joe said, "Hi, guys. We're just about to get into some of the tactics that we can use to correct one of the 'repulsive feelings' we've been creating among our customers. After that we're going to see if we can do something about Bill's ties." Bill was known for his loud, colorful ties. The entire ICE team, including Bill, roared with laughter. The fun was back at Tanner Enterprises.

"Never mind my ties," countered Bill. He handled the bright silk image of Mickey and Minnie Mouse that he had chosen to wear that day. "I love my ties. And besides, if I stop wearing 'em, you'll have to find something else to laugh at." Bill looked directly at Chelsea and Sara. "We're kind of jumping around here a little. Is that okay?"

"Certainly," answered Sara. "ICE is designed to allow you to move back and forth, to create an 'ICE-flow,' as it were." Everyone groaned.

Joe said, "I bet that's not the first time you've used that line."

"I'm afraid not," she replied.

Bill took a moment to explain to the two new arrivals the context in which they were asking the question projected on the screen, then turned to the ICE team.

"So, what can we do to correct the repulsive feelings we create when we don't live up to our 'quality' value?"

"Aren't we really asking ourselves what we have to do to ensure we always deliver quality?" asked Elaine.

"That's right," replied Sara. "In this particular example, you need to develop a list of things that you can do to ensure you live up to the value of 'quality is not an option.'"

"Who wants to start?" asked Joe.

"Why don't *we* start by dropping a third of our product line?" suggested Karen.

"Really?" asked Bill. "Why do you think that would help us?"

"We carry close to forty products now and, even though we're supposed to be an 'inbound-outbound' call center, we spend all our time handling inbound calls. Most of these calls are from unhappy customers, and I'd say that over two-thirds of them are from customers who use the same twelve or thirteen products. We rarely get the chance to call out, which is why our upgrade sales are so low. The sales we do make are really no more than a reflection of the orders we take when customers call us. And of course we never make a sale when a customer calls us with a complaint."

"The same twelve or thirteen products are causing all the complaints?" asked Elaine.

"Definitely. The 'In Touch' products are a disaster. That portfolio alone represents ten products. There are also a couple of dogs in the new 'Infinity' line, but the complaints seem to be lessening there."

"Elaine, what do our financials look like for the 'In Touch' product line?" asked Bill.

"Well, now I'm not sure. Our current view is that we're breaking even on the 'In Touch' line and we were even projecting a small profit next year. We're a little behind on revenues from what we'd forecast in the business plan, but not to a level where we were re-evaluating the product line."

"How will Karen's ICE change our current financial assessment of this product line?"

"We have eighty people in our call center. Today we transfer costs to our product lines on an allocation basis."

"Meaning?" asked Chelsea.

"Meaning that we allocate the loaded costs for the entire call center equally across the four product lines we offer and that they support. This means that the 'In Touch' income statement reflects approximately twenty-five percent of the call center operations costs —"

"Instead of the sixty percent that it should be reflecting," added Bill. "Joe, off the top of my head, it seems we're losing millions of dollars annually on the 'In Touch' line."

Joe agreed. "If we close it down —"

"We'd have more time to sell," added Karen.

"Karen, how much more business do you think the call center could generate?" asked Elaine.

"If the 'In Touch' line was killed, probably another hundred thousand dollars a year per rep."

The implications of the ICE they had received from Karen were enormous. Killing a money-losing product line and redirecting the support resources to proactive, revenue-generating activity would yield a huge financial return for Tanner. Joe quickly did the math in his head. He looked directly at Bill and said softly, "Breakthrough."

Managing
Human Resources

*A*s Sara, Chelsea, and Joe exited the conference room, they almost bumped into Joe's assistant, Rachel. And to Sara's surprise, Wally was with her. "Oh! Hi, boss. I didn't expect to see you here today."

"I hadn't planned on it, but Joe called me about forty minutes ago to tell me he really believed that some breakthrough thinking was taking place. His enthusiasm was infectious, so I decided to pop over and check things out for myself."

"Has it only been forty minutes?" asked Joe incredulously. "I've been moving around from session to session, and it's hard to believe that I've heard so many exciting ideas in such a short time. Right now, for example, the marketing team is working on a whole new way to electronically distribute software upgrades to our major clients. It has the potential to greatly reduce our distribution costs, and also increase sales."

"I haven't seen the people in our company this energized in years."

"Neither have I, Chelsea," agreed Joe.

"Where are you three going now?" asked Wally.

"We thought we'd see how the human resources ICE team is doing," replied Joe.

"Sounds good," said Wally. "Mind if I join you?"

The human resources ICE session was being led jointly by Dyson Lane and her Walden Chase ICE assistant, Tim Davis. Joe and his colleagues quietly entered the room and sat down at the back. The ICE team was so involved in the dialogue that they barely noticed the interruption. That was a good sign, Joe concluded.

"So, before we ask ourselves how we can eliminate the presence of strategic avoidance Values/Feelings,

---

HR STRATEGIC AVOIDANCE
VALUE/FEELING CONCEPT DEVELOPMENT

What values must the company avoid to prevent instilling negative feelings in its employees that will erode employee confidence in and loyalty to the company?

VALUES	FEELINGS
Employees are expendable	Disloyal
Do as you're told	Disrespected
Information is power	Directionless
Hierarchy defines success	Intimidated
Under pay and over work	Used
Policy rules	Stifled
Training is a privilege	Underdeveloped
Ignore success; punish failure	Risk-adverse; angry

let's review our map 4 Concept Development chart for our visitors.

"As you can see," Tim continued, "we were able to define a whole lot of values that we need to avoid displaying. Otherwise, we'll generate the wrong kinds of feelings among our employee base. Our task now is to answer this question: What can we do to eliminate the application of strategic avoidance values and prevent bringing out negative feelings in our employees?"

"Any suggestions as to which negative value we should focus on first?" asked Dyson.

"How about overworked and underpaid? That pretty well sums up my life, and I'd like to know what you're going to do about it," shouted Steve French, one of Tanner's systems engineers. His comment was greeted with warm laughter.

Dyson smiled. "You haven't been listening, Steve. This is not *my* problem anymore. It belongs to the entire ICE team. Sara, I really like this part of the system."

Steve interjected, "Okay, how about we give everybody twenty percent raises and stock options?"

There was a chorus of support for Steve's suggestion and many of the ICE team turned to look at Joe. Dyson picked up on the energy in the room. "What do you say, Joe? Steve might be on to something."

Joe chuckled. "Hey, as long as I can get in on the action, I'm all for it." Everyone laughed. "I recognize that you're mostly having some fun, but there's probably a real issue here. Steve, you started this, and

I suspect there are some negative feelings that exist within the organization linked to our not living up to our 'pay for performance' value. Can you elaborate?"

"Well, I can only speak for my area, but I believe that we're not paying our systems engineers at market right now —"

"Steve, I have benchmarking data that confirms that we are, in fact, paying —"

"Dyson, sorry," said Joe, "I don't mean to cut you off, but let's hear Steve out before we introduce our benchmarking data." He turned to Steve. "Maybe our benchmarking is not giving us the complete picture."

"Thanks, Joe. I think you're right. I mean, I don't think the surveys of other companies' salary levels are telling the whole story. There are a lot of areas of compensation we don't even touch."

"Can you give us some examples, Steve?" asked Dyson.

"Sure. First, I'm sure you know this, but in case you don't, you should be aware that we have experienced a forty percent turnover of staff in the systems engineering area in the past twelve months."

Joe was clearly surprised. "Really?" He looked at Dyson.

"You've got me on this one. I show our IT department experiencing a turnover rate of approximately sixteen percent, which is just slightly above industry standard."

"I'm sure that's true for the whole department, but that represents how many people — two hundred or so, right?" pointed out Steve.

"Approximately."

"We're only forty in systems engineering and we've lost sixteen people in the last twelve months."

"Why are we losing them?" asked Joe.

"Several reasons. First, the skills resident in this group are in really high demand right now. We are mostly enterprising network engineers with strong Internet skills. Companies are willing to pay more for this kind of expertise. Despite that, it's not really money that's the issue."

"What is the issue?" asked Dyson.

"A piece of the action. I think, without exception, every single engineer who has left has received stock options from their new employers. Some of them may never collect a nickel on them, but I know from talking to some of my former colleagues that they love the feeling of owning a piece of the company, and of working for an organization that is not afraid to share the wealth. The old days, when the only people who bene-fited from a company's wealth creation were the senior executives, are history. Today's new breed of companies recognizes that making the employees part-owners of the company creates loyalty. And because a lot of these options don't kick in for a year or two, they also have built in an incredible ability to retain employees. You just don't leave a company if there's a guaranteed payday down the road." Steve paused to let the impact of his words sink in. "We're not there yet. This may sound harsh, but there's a little too much 'old-think' around here. The rules of the game have changed. We need to step up."

"Dyson, what does it cost us when we lose an employee?" asked Joe.

"It depends on the area of the business, of course, but I'd say our average training cost is in the neighborhood of $40,000 including salary paid during training. Then there are the intangible costs, like lost productivity."

"Not to mention the additional load that gets dumped on the people who haven't left, which, I guess, is the 'overworked' part of my comment," added Steve.

Sara said, "If I can just make a couple of comments. First, the input you are providing is excellent, and Dyson, you are doing a great job drawing out the strategic avoidance Values/Feelings. However, let's not forget that what we're trying to do here is avoid these negative values." Sara had seen this kind of thing happen before. New participants sometimes slipped into complain mode and, while that step was important, it often kept them from defining the actions necessary to address the problem. "Steve, what ICE can you give us that might help us correct this situation?"

Steve grinned. "Hey, I thought you'd never ask. . . ."

Joe had seen ICE applied at Tanner Enterprises for only a little over nine hours, but he was amazed at what he had learned about the tremendous expertise within his organization.

This time, the breakthrough thinking had come from Lana Burke, a junior manager in Tanner's HR department. "Dyson, Steve has some interesting ideas about compensation, but I think there might be another approach we could take."

"Great, Lana. What do you have in mind?"

Lana stepped over to the blackboard. "Well, I'm not an expert on compensation, by any means, but I did do my Master's thesis on corporate compensation and the role it plays in shaping this country's most successful companies . . ." She hesitated, clearly unsure of how best to proceed.

Dyson excitedly provided Lana with the encouragement she needed. "Take it away, Lana! What can you tell us?"

"I guess the first thing that comes to mind is that we have several different compensation models being applied throughout the company, and none of them are linked. This creates situations where whole departments can be in conflict with each other."

"Can you give us an example?" asked Sara.

"Sure. Our product managers are eligible for a bonus based on the financial performance of the products they represent. They can also earn incentive dollars by delivering their products to market on time, as defined in their original business plans."

"That's something I never thought of," interjected Joe. "Should they be paid based on the timing in their plans?"

"It's usually okay, since the plans are subject to senior management approval. The real problem, however, is that their compensation is not linked to the service performance of the product, unlike the bonuses of our customer service representatives, which are linked 100% to customer satisfaction."

"I see what you're getting at, Lana. If the product managers release a poor quality product, they might be affected financially if the revenues don't accrue as a result, but the customer service team will definitely feel the pinch," said Dyson.

"Right."

"So how do we fix this?"

"By implementing a company-wide compensation model that employs factoring." Lana saw the blank stares around the room. "Let me explain.

"Say I'm a product manager. My product gets released early and is delivering the financial performance I committed to in my business plan. Under my current compensation formula, I have earned an annual bonus of, let's say, $30,000, or 120% of my on-plan earning potential. I'll write it down to make it clearer."

Position	Salary	Bonus-financials (120%)	Bonus-product intro (120%)	Total
pr. mgr.	$50K	$20K	$10K	$80K

"So, I've earned $80K. Okay, now I'm a customer service representative. The product we've just released is welcomed by the marketplace. Sales are great, everybody's happy, but soon the customer service calls start pouring in because the product is just not robust enough."

"It was released too early," said Steve.

"Exactly. Now the product manager gets his or her bonus. No problem there. But the poor customer service representative's bonus is determined based on our customer satisfaction indices. And since our customers are not happy, the rep's bonus opportunity is severely compromised. It might look like this."

Position	Salary	Bonus-Customer Service (25%)	Total
cust. service rep.	$30K	$1.5K	$31.5K

"So, one department's behavior, motivated by its compensation opportunity, negatively affects the opportunity of another," said Joe.

"Right. Factoring fixes that. In this example, simply take the bonus earned by the product manager and factor it based on the percent bonus earned by the customer service rep, and vice-versa."

Position	Salary	Bonus earned	X Customer Service factor	Total Bonus
pr. mgr.	$50K	$30K	0.25	$7.5K

"Ouch," said Steve.

"Exactly. But what you have to ask yourself is what kind of behavior this would drive," replied Lana.

"I certainly wouldn't be releasing products before they were ready."

"Right. And there's an upside here, of course. If the customer service indices delivered a bonus of, say, 120%, then the product manager would receive 120% of his $30,000, or an additional $6,000 bonus."

"I like it," said Joe. "Factoring would really bring the various departments together and would certainly foster a teamwork attitude."

"You're right, Joe. My thesis suggests that this kind of compensation model would really unify a company."

"Any other ICE you can give us, Lana?" asked Sara.

"Yes. I believe we need to consider making stock options available to all employees. These would be non-voting shares and would only become fully vested two years after their date of issue, and only if the recipients were still employees of the company. Implementing an employee stock option plan would help solve Tanner's employee attrition problem and create long-term loyalty to the company that doesn't exist today."

"Lana, I think what you're suggesting is brilliant, and I don't see why we can't pursue this kind of thinking."

"Thanks, Joe."

"Dyson, do you have any concerns?"

"None, although I have to admit that I'm a little embarrassed to find out that an expert on compensation is working within my department and I wasn't aware of it."

"Don't be," Sara volunteered. "If you knew where every source of expertise resided within your organization, you wouldn't need ICE. This kind of revelation is very common. One of the first times I ran an ICE session I discovered that we had one of the top environmentalists in the country working for us. She was heavily involved with Greenpeace, and she helped us correct a number of environmentally sensitive negative feelings we had been creating within a particular community. It was amazing."

"*ICE* is amazing," said Joe. "And so are you, Lana. Thank you."

The team moved onto the next Strategic Avoidance Value/Feeling map, and Joe, Wally, Sara, and Chelsea slipped out of the room. It was clear to each of them that ICE was about to change the face of human resources at Tanner Enterprises.

10

Operational Excellence

*I*n the corridor outside the conference room, Joe turned to Wally. "This is unbelievable. I feel like we're going through a corporate rebirth in a single day."

"That's a good way to describe what's happening, Joe. But like any birth, delivering the baby safely is only the first step in the process of raising a strong, healthy child and producing an independent, contributing adult."

"Wally's right," added Sara. "The key to ICE, and to Tanner's future, is to ensure that the tactics developed through ICE are put into place."

"And ICE must be applied continuously throughout the process," said Wally. "It has to become part of your culture for you to achieve the long-term benefits of the program."

"And to realize long-term benefits for your company and its people," said Sara.

Joe nodded. What Wally and Sara were saying made sense. And from what Joe had observed so far, it wouldn't require much convincing for the people of Tanner to adopt ICE as their own secret weapon.

"Where are you guys off to now?" asked Chelsea.

"I think I'm going to head over to operations and see how they're making out," said Joe. "How about you guys?"

"We have to start plugging some information into the presentation framework we're going to be using tomorrow. I think we have enough to get started," replied Sara.

"I've seen enough to know ICE is delivering what Tanner needs right now, Joe. I'm going to head out but I'll be back later this evening to review your presentation if that's okay."

"Of course, Wally," replied Joe. "We'll benefit from your input."

The operations team was one of the larger ICE squads assembled, so upon joining the meeting, Joe was surprised to see that the team had already completed the four-stage ICE map development process. Joe took a seat at the back of the room as his vice-president of operations, Stan Krupski, addressed the group.

". . . record time, according to Paula." Stan half bowed to his Walden Chase ICE consultant. "We couldn't have gotten this far so quickly without you. Gang, how about a big round of applause for our new friend?"

Paula quietly acknowledged their appreciation.

Once the room quieted, Stan continued. "You may have noticed that the big guy himself has joined our meeting. And, as usual, his timing is impeccable. Joe, we're about to summarize the high-level tactics that we've developed through ICE. Once that's done, Kent Waters is going to do some number crunching for us to see what kind of financial impact the implementation of our tactical plan will have on the business. This, of course, will be the view from 'fifty thousand feet.' It will have to be better defined and quantified, but it should give you the information you need to address our immediate circumstances."

"That's great, Stan. Fire away."

"Okay." Stan moved to the slide projector. "Paula was kind enough to produce this summary for us while we took our last break." He slid the acetate onto the overhead projector.

Tanner's Five Steps to Operational Excellence
- *Upgrade shop-floor wiring infrastructure*
- *Outsource acceptance testing*
- *Implement 'just-in-time' inventory with suppliers*
- *Deploy remote diagnostics capability*
- *Implement "zero down-time" incentive plan*

"The first tactic, upgrading our infrastructure, requires some capital expenditure, but the team believes that the payback will be achieved in less than six months." Stan addressed Don Brewer, one of his ICE team. "Don, since this tactic was a product of your ICE, could you elaborate on this point for Joe?"

"Oh, sure. Joe, we've done a really good job in upgrading our assembly processes. Our computing power is second to none, and we have all the latest robotics tools. Our problem is with our factory wiring. It's all analog-based and we're operating in a digital world. We —"

"Whoa, Don," Joe interrupted, smiling. "How about some plain English for me here?"

Don laughed. "Okay. The information, or data, that flows through the factory and makes everything work moves too slowly. We have really fast technology that has the power to speed up our assembly process and produce probably forty percent more product per day if we had new wiring to provide us with better band-width."

"Bandwidth?"

"Think of it as the size of the pipe that connects all of our computers and robots. We have a garden hose and we need a fire hose to be more productive.

"There are a couple of huge benefits here, Joe. Number one is that our per-unit production costs would drop dramatically, allowing us to lower prices somewhat and increase our margins. And second, the extra production capability we'd gain here would allow us to discontinue production at one of our other sites."

"That would represent a huge savings to us," mar-velled Joe.

"Finance is working the numbers as we speak," said Don.

"This is terrific. How about the second ICE tactic?" asked Joe.

"Outsource acceptance testing? This one was a real revelation to me. Colin, can you cover this one?"

"Sure. We have highly skilled, well-paid engineers doing acceptance testing. I think we counted about ten testers in this facility alone and Stan confirmed that we have close to thirty engineers in the company doing this. The work is important, but it doesn't require the kind of skill-set we're deploying. I think we could outsource this work and take significant cost out of the business."

"We also have extremely high turnover in this area of the business," said Stan, referring to his notes. "Forty percent in the last year."

"The guys doing this are bored to tears," added Colin. "They didn't study computer engineering or computer science to become acceptance testers."

"This makes a lot of sense," replied Joe, "but what about the people who are in those jobs today? If we outsource, are we not looking at laying off the incumbents?"

"Their raw skills are in big demand," answered Colin. "We could engage a placement firm to ease the transition of these people into new jobs and implement our outsourcing over time as we experience or cause attrition."

"We think that it would take six months," added Stan. "And the bottom line would be a thirty-percent savings in our labor costs, with no loss of quality. Maybe even an improvement."

"I like it," said Joe. "What about your third tactic?"

"This one's a no-brainer," replied Stan. "Today, we have raw materials that sit in our warehouses for weeks, or even months sometimes, waiting to be used in our manufacturing processes. We have fourteen primary suppliers. What's been suggested by Stacy here is that we establish electronic connections with our suppliers, which will trigger orders to them when we need more materials. They would deliver it to us 'just in time' for us to use it. The carrying costs we absorb when their products sit in our warehouses would disappear."

"How much —"

"Finance is —"

"Working on it." Joe was getting used to this routine.

"That's right," chuckled Stan. "And for the record, Stacy's ICE stems from her previous experience with an electronic commerce company that specializes in supply-chain integration. So she has the contacts in the industry to help us make this happen quickly."

"That's terrific. Congratulations, Stacy. This is an excellent idea."

Stan continued. "The remote diagnostics tactic is an interesting one. Several members of the team provided ICE on this one. The consensus is that we could reduce our on-premises service calls by close to twenty-five percent if we acquired the right remote diagnostic tools."

"Really?"

Ahmed, one of the ICE team, answered this time. "Our products are deployed on computer platforms. Everything from PCs right through to servers and mainframes. I won't get technical on you here, but in today's world, all of these things are connected to a network of some kind, including the Internet. That means we can connect to these devices. With the right tools we could diagnose service problems remotely and, in many cases, upload or send the user the 'fix' they need electronically."

"Reducing costly service calls."

"Exactly. And increasing the efficiency of the service people."

"Over time we'd need fewer people," Joe concluded.

"Right."

"Wow. I'm impressed. Stan, how about the last tactic on your list?"

"This one received the most attention. Today we have 'up-time' on our assembly lines of 99.7%, which is about the industry standard. That 0.03% down-time, however, translates into a mean time between failure of fifty days, assuming a four-hour work production stoppage. We estimate that each period of down-time costs us $100,000 in lost production time. Seven down-time periods cost us $700,000. The proposal here is a simple one. Let's put an annual incentive in front of our operations department equal to half of what we can save the company by avoiding down-time. If we delivered zero down-time we'd pay out $350,000 in additional bonus to the members of the ops department."

"I love it," praised Joe. And he loved what ICE had done for Stan's department. He couldn't wait to see the estimated financial impact of their five-point tactical plan. It would clearly help the future for Tanner Enterprises become a little brighter.

11

Bringing It
All Together

*J*oe glanced at his watch. It was almost 4 A.M., but his energy level remained high. Joe knew why. Despite his recent efforts to personally energize his people and to fix Tanner Enterprises, Joe had resigned himself to the fact that his company would soon be bankrupt. Now, in less than three days, thanks to ICE, he had become convinced that the company could be saved. And not only could it be saved, it could thrive. The tactical plans that ICE had delivered through the various departmental sessions were brilliant. Joe scanned the room. Dyson Lane, Bill Conrad, Ben Riley, Jay Cameron, Kent Waters, Chelsea Bain, Walden "Wally" Chase, and Sara Daly. His senior executives, his good friend, and the ICE Queen. They were a good team, and even better people.

Joe listened as Chelsea walked everyone through the key elements in Tanner's turnaround strategy: streamlining the product line; segmenting the market; developing complementary sales channels; implementing an employee retention plan; supply-chain integration; outsourcing non-core business functions; upgrading the information technology infrastructure. The list was impressive.

As Chelsea finished the review, which she and Sara had structured into a slick presentation, the door opened and Bruna Lake joined the group. Bruna was one of the top financial analysts in Kent Waters's department, and she had been working diligently to recast Tanner's financial view in response to the ICE tactical plans.

"Ahh, Bruna. You're just in time," welcomed Chelsea.

"Good." Bruna moved smartly to the front of the room. She flipped a slide onto the projector and said, "Welcome to the new, improved Tanner Enterprises."

The "pin-drop" silence that ensued was followed by an outburst of enthusiastic energy as the members of the team absorbed what ICE had done for them. Tanner Enterprises, which was mired in debt, could be turned around within twelve months, provided the financiers were willing to give them the time to effect the changes. The company would return to profitability within eighteen months and would retire all of its short-term debt, and most of its long-term debt, within three years. The three-to-five year financial view painted a portrait of a company with healthy growth and a strong financial performance.

Joe let out a soft, low whistle. "Wow. This is an amazing picture. Guys, can we really do this?" He knew the answer before asking the question, but he needed to have his own beliefs affirmed by his senior executives. They answered at the same time.

"You bet we can!"

"Absolutely!"

"We'll do it, Joe!"

"Bet on it!"

"Of course!"

ICE had made believers of all of them. Joe glanced at his watch again. "I'm on in less than five hours. Thanks to each of you for all your efforts. This company is a big part of my life and . . ." His emotions spilled over but he held them in check. But his employees, his friends, sensed what he was feeling and knew how important Tanner Enterprises was to this man for whom they cared deeply. "Just . . . well, thanks. I won't let you down." He paused for a moment. "And Wally —"

"Save it, Joe. I told you earlier what can you do to thank me. Save the company."

Joe stopped talking for a moment to gather his thoughts. He had been on his feet for the past two hours, explaining to the three men and one woman who controlled the future of his company how he intended to resurrect Tanner Enterprises. He had refrained from mentioning ICE, choosing instead to focus on the key strategies and tactics that would be deployed in an effort to turn the company around. Joe's audience was a tough one, but he respected that. Their job was to protect the investments of their respective institutions and their shareholders, and if that meant forcing Tanner to declare bankruptcy, then so be it.

Joe took a sip of water, then continued. "Gentlemen, I think I've said enough at this stage. I believe I've described to you a concrete plan that will first get my company back on its feet, and second retire the debts we have accrued with each of your organizations. In doing so, we will deliver to you a solid return on your investments in Tanner Enterprises. I guess, at this point, the rest is up to you."

The eldest of the bankers, and the one whose firm had the most money invested in Joe's company, spoke first. "Joe, we've been having meetings like this every month for about a year now, and I have to confess that I came here today ready to make a decision to call in our loans, which you know would have forced you into receivership. I had talked to my esteemed colleagues here and we all pretty much agreed. That said, I've seen some new thinking here today and some plans for your company that, quite frankly, weren't in place one short month ago. I like what I've seen today. I'm not saying that I'm convinced that Tanner can survive, but I believe that it's worth the wait. As for me, I'm prepared to extend the financial support you require to get over your immediate cash crunch, and to stick with you for at least the next year or so, pending quarterly reviews that demonstrate you are delivering what you have committed to here today. Also . . ."

The banker droned on, stating the conditions of their ongoing support. His colleagues also lent their support to Joe's turnaround plan. Joe barely grasped what they were saying. He was exhausted and ecstatic, and all he wanted to do was race to the office and shout for all to hear that ICE had saved Tanner Enterprises.

Joe picked up his cell phone the moment he entered his vehicle and placed a call to the private line of the founder and chairman of one of the continent's most successful companies. Wally answered on the first ring. "Wally speaking."

"It's Joe. Remember what you wanted as your only thanks?"

"Yeah."

"Just say, 'You're welcome.'"

Epilogue:

Three Years of ICE

*J*oe Tanner needed a workout. His company, Tanner Enterprises, had just recorded its most successful year in its history, thanks to the phenomenal success of its new product line and a series of synergistic acquisitions. Later in the evening, Joe was being presented with the CEO-of-the-Year award, at an event sponsored by one of the nation's largest business associations. The award was an incredible honor, and Joe was thrilled to receive it on behalf of his flourishing company.

As Joe worked away on the Lifecycle, he noticed one of his squash buddies, Ryan Nelson, working out nearby. Ryan, who was always cheerful, seemed rather down. In fact, Ryan had not even noticed Joe exercising.

Joe got off the stationary bike and walked over to Ryan, who was sitting on one of the exercise benches.

"Hey, Ryan? What's up?"

Ryan looked up. "Oh, hi, Joe. Not much."

"Hey, Ryan, I've known you long enough to know that something isn't right. Are you sure things are okay?"

"Well, it's nothing you can help with, really. My company's going through a really tough time and I'm not sure we're going to survive. You know how it is."

Joe smiled. His mind raced back to a similar conversation he had in the same place three years before. He thought of Wally and of Sara and of the tremendous people at Walden Chase.

"Ryan, my friend, I think what you need to do right now is to apply a little ICE."